Jesus Christ Is Risen Today!

The story of Easter from Matthew 28;
Mark 16; Luke 24; John 20 for children

Eric C. Bohnet
Illustrated by Erika LeBarre

CONCORDIA PUBLISHING HOUSE · SAINT LOUIS

We went to His tomb this morning,
and the stone was rolled away.
We saw the truth we soon would know:
Jesus Christ is ris'n today.

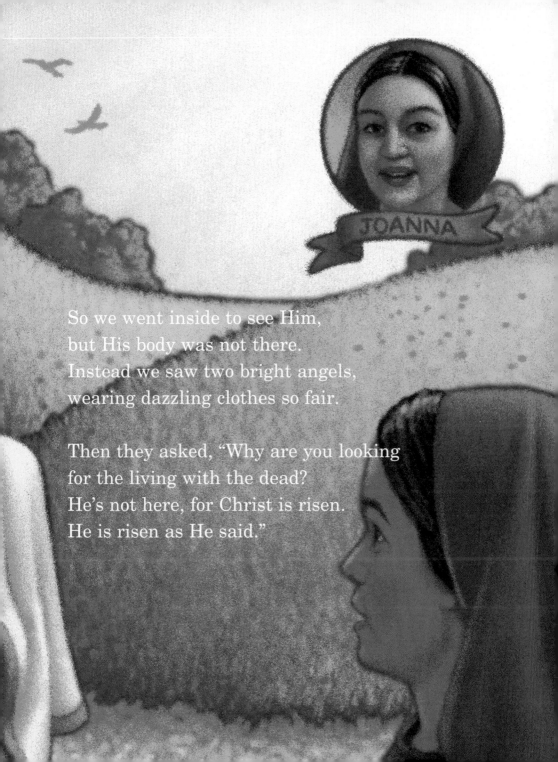

JOANNA

So we went inside to see Him,
but His body was not there.
Instead we saw two bright angels,
wearing dazzling clothes so fair.

Then they asked, "Why are you looking
for the living with the dead?
He's not here, for Christ is risen.
He is risen as He said."

I saw the stone gone with the rest,
but I ran away in fear.
I told Peter—he went back there,
but my eyes were filled with tears.

I went back to look for Jesus,
for I could not stay away.
Then I saw Him. He said, "Mary,"
and I knew He'd ris'n today.

MARY MAGDALENE

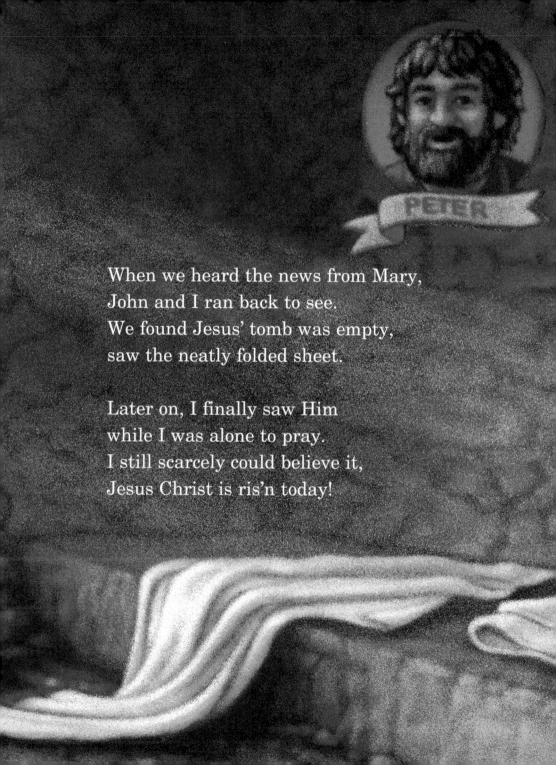

When we heard the news from Mary,
John and I ran back to see.
We found Jesus' tomb was empty,
saw the neatly folded sheet.

Later on, I finally saw Him
while I was alone to pray.
I still scarcely could believe it,
Jesus Christ is ris'n today!

CLEOPAS

We were walking to Emmaus,
talking of all that had passed.
Then we were joined by a stranger
who explained it all at last.

"Look at Moses and the Prophets,
what they wrote about the Christ.
He would die and greatly suffer—
that's how He'd pay sin's great price."

Oh, our hearts they burned within us
as He opened up our eyes.
For He taught us from the Scriptures
how the Christ would die and rise.

CLEOPAS

We invited Him to dinner,
and He blessed and broke the bread.
Then He vanished, but we saw that
it was Jesus, no more dead.

To Jerusalem we hurried,
even ran most of the way.
We brought the good news to our friends:
Jesus Christ is ris'n today.

The disciples were all hiding
in Jerusalem that night.
They told me Jesus came to them,
but I doubted without sight.

Then He was with us once again.
"Peace to you" is what He said.
"See My hands and feet and touch Me,
for I am no longer dead."

"It was written I would suffer
and the third day rise again.
Now I send you to the whole world;
there's forgiveness in My name."

'Twas the greatest vict'ry ever;
death and sin would go away.
Tell the world! It needs to hear it:
"Jesus Christ is ris'n today!"

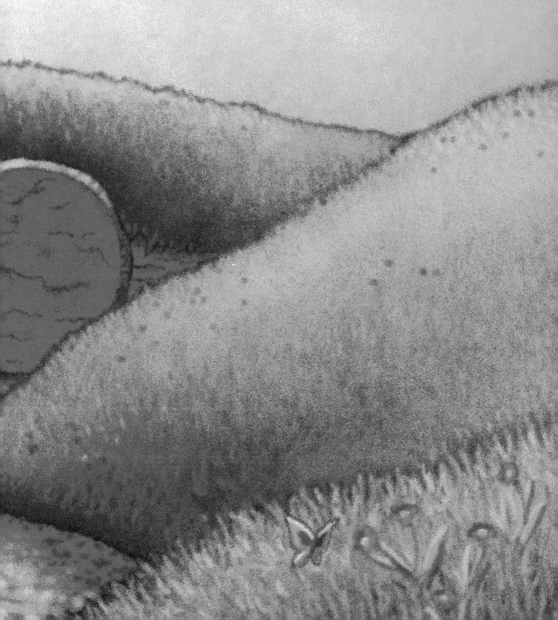

Dear Parent,

The Easter hymn "Jesus Christ Is Risen Today" dates back centuries. An older version can be traced to the early 1400s. Variations of the version we sing today have been published in hymnals since the early 1700s. It is included in hundreds of hymnals and is known to Christians everywhere.

We sing this hymn with great joy as we celebrate our Lord's resurrection and rejoice in His victory over sin, death, and the devil. The hymn's simple words express the Gospel beautifully: Jesus Christ, "who endured the cross and grave, Alleluia! Sinners to redeem and save. Alleluia!"

Easter, retold in this book through the words of people who were with Jesus at His death and after His resurrection, is the fulfillment of God's promise in Genesis 3:15 to crush sin and send the Offspring of Eve ("the mother of all living" [Genesis 3:20]) to do it. As you read this book with your little one, remind him or her that we celebrate Christmas because that is when our Savior was born. We observe Good Friday because that is when Jesus' work of taking on the sin of the world was completed. And we celebrate Easter because that is when our Savior rose from the grave to eternal life so that we may have eternal life through Him. Jesus Christ is risen today! Alleluia!

The editor